D0478502

A start me up Book

Dinosaurs

By Joachim Oppermann

Illustrated by Manfred Rohrbeck

*The largest complete skeleton of a giant sauropod
was discovered in East Africa in 1910 and reconstructed
in the Natural History Museum, Berlin, Germany.*

Tessloff Publishing

Preface

Dinosaur — the word itself stirs our imagination. For most people, it suggests images of giant prehistoric animals with fantastic characteristics. Imaginative books and articles, vividly colored pictures, and spectacular exhibits with moving, roaring dinosaur robots give us an ever more dazzling impression of the great variety of these animals.

The last dinosaurs died 65 million years ago, however, and no one has ever seen a living one. No one can reliably describe their colors or tell us what they ate. Only a few parts and traces of their bodies remain: fossilized bones and eggs, footprints and skin impressions. Despite patient detective work, there is still a lot that we do not know about them. Attempts to complete our picture of them with new explanations and theories require both imagination and caution.

When they make new discoveries, scientists often have to correct previous assumptions because of the new evidence. Over the past 10 years numerous discoveries have substantially changed and expanded our complicated picture of the dinosaur world.

This **start me up!**™ book recounts the origin, appearance, and way of life of more than sixty of the best-known dinosaur species.

Volume 2

PUBLISHERS: Tessloff Publishing, Quadrillion Media LLC

EDITOR: Alan Swensen

PICTURE SOURCES: Bayer. Staatssammlung für Palaeontologie und hist. Geologie, Munich: p. 6; Dr. Martin Lockley, University of Colorado at Denver: p. 41; Museum für Naturkunde, Berlin: pp. 1, 6, 20, 46; Natural History Museum, London: pp. 6, 29, 34, 36, 40; Novosti Photo Library, London: p. 6

ILLUSTRATIONS: Manfred Rohrbeck

Translated by William Connors and Richard Dennis

COPYRIGHT: © MCMXCVIII Tessloff Publishing, Burgschmietstrasse 2-4, 90419 Nuremberg, Germany
© MCMXCVIII Quadrillion Media LLC, 10105 East Via Linda Road, Suite 103-390, Scottsdale AZ 85258, USA

Visit us on the World Wide Web at http://www.quadrillionusa.com

All rights reserved. No part of this book may be reproduced or transmitted in any form or by any means, electronic or mechanical, including photocopy, recording or any information storage and retrieval systems, without written permission from the publisher, except by a reviewer who may quote brief passages in a review.

Library of Congress Cataloging-in-Publication Data is available.

ISBN 1-58185-001-8

Printed in Belgium

Printing 10 9 8 7 6 5 4 3 2 1

Contents

A Short History of Dinosaur Fossil Finds

Were the dragons in fairy tales and myths large prehistoric reptiles?

It has been less than 200 years since scientists first reported finding unusual fossilized bones or teeth. These early discoveries were surely not the first time people found such fossils, however. People long ago must have come across fossilized bones and teeth when they were plowing fields or mining for precious metals, or when they were digging wells or foundations for buildings. These strange, gigantic bones may have inspired the many fairy tales and myths about dragons and mythical beasts.

Stories of dragons or huge reptiles are found in many cultures. In the famous Greek myth of Jason and the Argonauts, a dragon guarded the Golden Fleece that Jason stole. Dragons also play an important role in ancient Chinese myths. There are also many cultures that once believed in giant serpent gods. Did these people think that the giant bones and teeth they found came from gods shaped like snakes? We don't really know, since there is no historical evidence we can examine. The first recorded fossil finds come from the 19th century.

THE FAIRY TALES and legends of cultures throughout the world tell of dragons and other fantastical creatures. The Chinese dragon legends are over 3,000 years old. The Toltecs of Central America worshipped the god Quetzalcoatl, the "Plumed Serpent."

"Fighting with the dragon"

Around 1820, discoveries of large, fossilized teeth and bones aroused the interest of English and French scientists. They gradually realized that such large bones could only have come from very large reptiles that had lived a

When did people realize what dinosaur bones were?

long time ago. In 1822 the English physician James Parkinson examined some fossils from the collection of a geologist named William Buckland. He recognized that the bones came from a very large animal that no longer existed. He gave this animal the name Megalosaurus, which means "great lizard." In 1824 Buckland himself began a project of describing the items in his collection and giving them scientific names. This was the first time that scholars recognized what dinosaur bones were and gave them fitting names.

The English physician Gideon Mantell reported a second exciting find in 1825. Three years earlier his wife, Mary, had discovered large teeth in a rock at the side of the road. Other teeth and fossilized bones were found in a quarry nearby. Because the teeth were shaped like those of an iguana, a Central and South American lizard, Mantell called the newly discovered animal Iguanodon or "iguana tooth."

EARLY FOSSIL FINDS AND IMAGES OF DINOSAURS

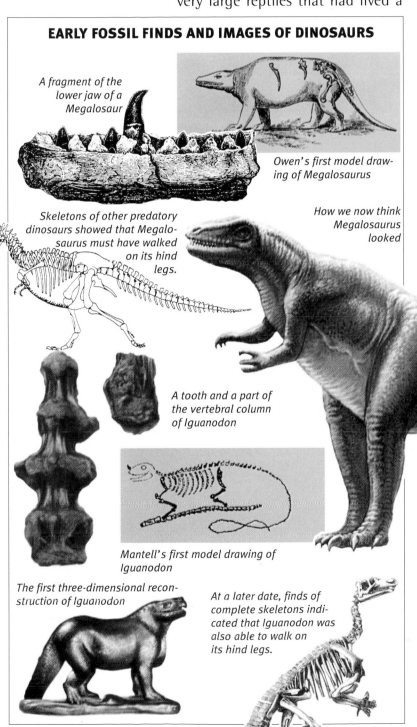

A fragment of the lower jaw of a Megalosaur

Owen's first model drawing of Megalosaurus

Skeletons of other predatory dinosaurs showed that Megalosaurus must have walked on its hind legs.

How we now think Megalosaurus looked

A tooth and a part of the vertebral column of Iguanodon

Mantell's first model drawing of Iguanodon

The first three-dimensional reconstruction of Iguanodon

At a later date, finds of complete skeletons indicated that Iguanodon was also able to walk on its hind legs.

These first discoveries were based on very little evidence — only a few bones or teeth. None of these researchers recognized yet that the newly discovered animals might be a completely different type of reptile. Professor Richard Owen in London was the first to realize this, but only after more complete remains had been found. He proposed calling all members of this reptile group "dinosaurs." The name "dinosaur" means "terrible lizard."

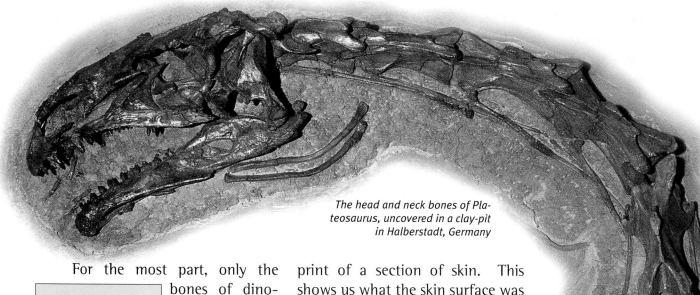

The head and neck bones of Plateosaurus, uncovered in a clay-pit in Halberstadt, Germany

What parts of the dinosaurs are left?

For the most part, only the bones of dinosaurs have been preserved. Complete skeletons or skulls with teeth are rare, and scientists feel very lucky when they find such fossils. Usually paleontologists (paleontology is the science that studies fossils of extinct plants and animals) have only bone fragments or individual teeth to work with.

Soft body tissue did not survive, but we sometimes find a clear imprint of a section of skin. This shows us what the skin surface was like. Discoveries of fossilized dinosaur eggs or bits of shells are always a great sensation, but unfortunately we can only guess which species they belong to. Even when there is a complete nest with eggs and a skeleton above it, we cannot be sure if the eggs are really from the same species as the skeleton. The skeleton might belong to another dinosaur that was robbing the nest.

Fossilized food found in the stomach region of a dinosaur skeleton is especially interesting. An example are the bones of a lizard found between the ribs of a small meat-eating dinosaur, Compsognathus. Fossilized dinosaur droppings also tell us a lot about the food dinosaurs ate.

Footprints and trails of footprints are very valuable, since they can provide information about the way of life, running speed and body size of the animals.

Fossilized claw bones, teeth, and eggs of dinosaurs.

A slab of limestone containing a skeleton of the smallest predatory dinosaur, Compsognathus. The bones of a lizard (its prey) are visible in the stomach region.

THE COMPLETE TWO-PART NAME is normally only used in scientific works. Otherwise the genus name suffices. When it is used as the name of a *type* of dinosaur, it is capitalized: "Tyrannosaurus was a meat-eater." When it refers to specific animals of the type, however, it is not usually capitalized: "Three tyrannosauruses attacked the grazing apatosauruses."

Discoveries of dinosaurs from the:

■ *Triassic Period*
250 million years ago

▲ *Jurassic Period*
205 to 135 million years ago

● *Cretaceous Period*
135 to 65 million years ago

Why do dinosaurs have such strange names?

Whenever a new type of dinosaur is discovered it is given its own name. The scientist who first studied the fossils and recognized that they did not belong to a known species has the right to christen the new dinosaur. The name becomes official when it is published in a scientific journal.

The name is always made of two parts: a genus name and a species name — the genus name is capitalized. In keeping with scientific tradition the names are in Latin. These Latin names are often formed from Greek words, geographic names, and also proper names. The name usually describes a typical characteristic of the dinosaur species. Stegosaurus armatus means "armored roof lizard" and refers to the typical plates along the back of the animal — scientists first thought these plates covered the animal like scales or shingles. Ceratosaurus nasicornis means "horn-lizard with a horn on its snout."

The name is sometimes formed from the place of discovery. Mamenchisaurus hochuanensis is made from Mamenchi and Hochuan, the discovery site and region in China. Lesothosaurus was found in Lesotho, Africa and Albertosaurus in Alberta, Canada.

Sometimes dinosaurs are named in honor of people who have made great contributions to research. Megalosaurus bucklandi and Iguanodon mantelli were named after the two English dinosaur researchers Mantell and Buckland. The small gazelle dinosaur Othniella was named after the American paleontologist, Othniel Charles Marsh, and the giant dinosaur Janenschia was named after the German researcher Werner Janensch. Janensch honored the Director of the Berlin Museum of Natural History, Wilhelm von Branca, by giving the name Brachiosaurus brancai (= Branca's arm lizard) to the largest of the giant dinosaurs.

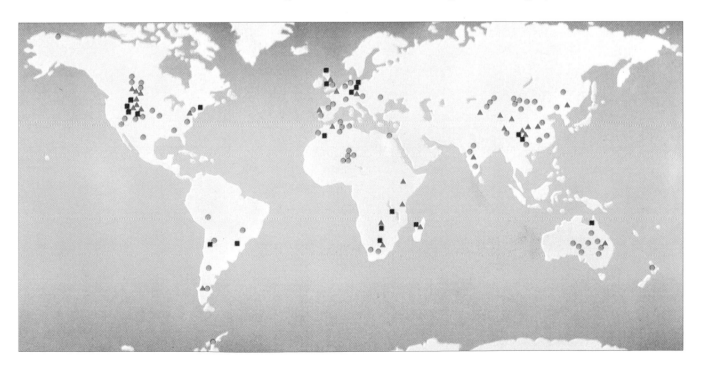

The Age of Dinosaurs

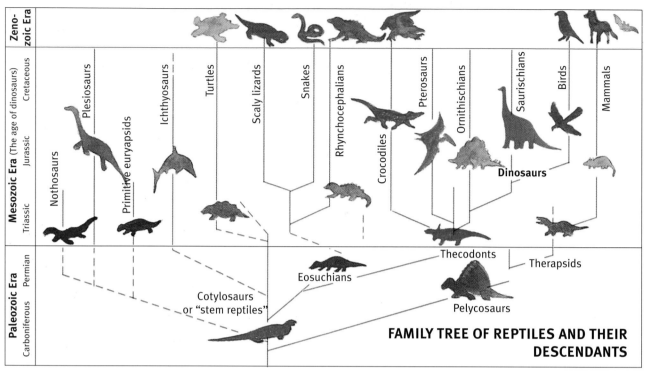

FAMILY TREE OF REPTILES AND THEIR DESCENDANTS

DINOSAUR GROUPS

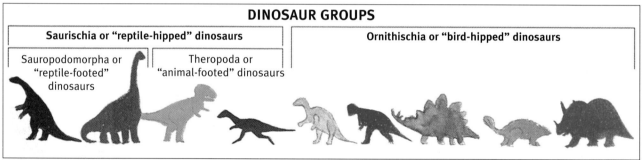

Saurischia or "reptile-hipped" dinosaurs				Ornithischia or "bird-hipped" dinosaurs					
Sauropodomorpha or "reptile-footed" dinosaurs		Theropoda or "animal-footed" dinosaurs							
Prosauropoda, ancestors of sauropods	Sauropoda	Carnosauria, large predatory dinosaurs	Coelurosauria, small predatory dinosaurs	Ornithopoda or "bird-footed" dinosaurs	Pachycephalosauria or "dome-headed" dinosaurs	Stegosauria or "plated" dinosaurs	Ankylosauria or "armored" dinosaurs	Ceratopsia or "horn-faced" dinosaurs

---

What were the dinosaurs?

The term "dinosaur" refers to one specific group of reptiles that lived in the Mesozoic Era. Besides the dinosaurs there were also many other "saurian" groups. Among the dinosaurs themselves there were also great differences, and it is often difficult to recognize the relationships among them. They ranged from species the size of cats or chickens to ones the size of whales; from species that moved on four legs to species that traveled on their hind legs; from nimble hunters and greedy meat-eaters to slow-moving plant-eaters. Still, the most important characteristic they all shared is one we can see in their physical appearance: their legs were positioned beneath their bodies and did not stick out to the sides as with most other reptiles. Because of this we could also call dinosaurs "walking saurians."

BESIDE THE DINOSAURS ("terrible" saurians) there were also many other types of saurians, such as pterosaurs ("flying" saurians), ichthyosaurs ("fish" saurians), crocodiles, and mammal-like reptiles. You can read more about them on pages 42–45.

From which animals did the dinosaurs descend?

The first real land vertebrates — vertebrates are animals with a backbone — were the cotylosaurs or "stem reptiles" (other reptiles "stem" from them). They evolved more than 300 million years ago. Unlike amphibians, they laid their eggs on land. When the egg hatched, a small, fully formed reptile emerged — not a larva or tadpole, as with amphibians.

The cotylosaur Hylonomus

These first lizard-sized land animals were the ancestors of all later reptiles. They soon adapted to different environments: carnivores and herbivores, crawlers and runners, forest and swamp dwellers. At least six different reptile groups developed in this way. The crocodile-like thecodonts ("socket-toothed" reptiles) were one group. They were from three to six feet long and were meat-eaters. They hunted insects, frogs, and small lizards. A few were able to lift themselves up and run on their hind legs.

This gave them a great advantage over reptile groups that had legs attached to their sides and moved on all fours. Scientists think this fast-running type of thecodont was the ancestor of the dinosaurs.

How many dinosaur species do we know of?

Well over 10,000 dinosaur remains have been found so far. They include individual bones and complete skeletons, skulls and teeth, eggs and droppings, fossilized footprints and skin impressions. Everything we know about dinosaurs was learned from these remains.

It has been more than 150 years since the first fossils were found, and since then paleontologists have identified and described more than 500 dinosaur species.

Some of these 500 species are so closely related that they are grouped together in a genus. Today we include nine species of horned dinosaurs in the genus Triceratops (= three-horn face). Some of the genera ("genera" is the plural form of "genus") are also gathered into larger groupings called infraorders, suborders, or orders — altogether there are more than 40 genera in the infraorder Sauropoda.

THE DINOSAUR GROUPS

with the most species were the carnosaurs (= predatory dinosaurs) with more than 150 genera, and the ornithopods (= "bird-footed" dinosaurs) that ran on two legs, with 65 genera. The stegosaurs were probably the group with the fewest members. Scientists have identified only 11 genera of stegosaurs.

The socket-toothed reptile Euparkeria

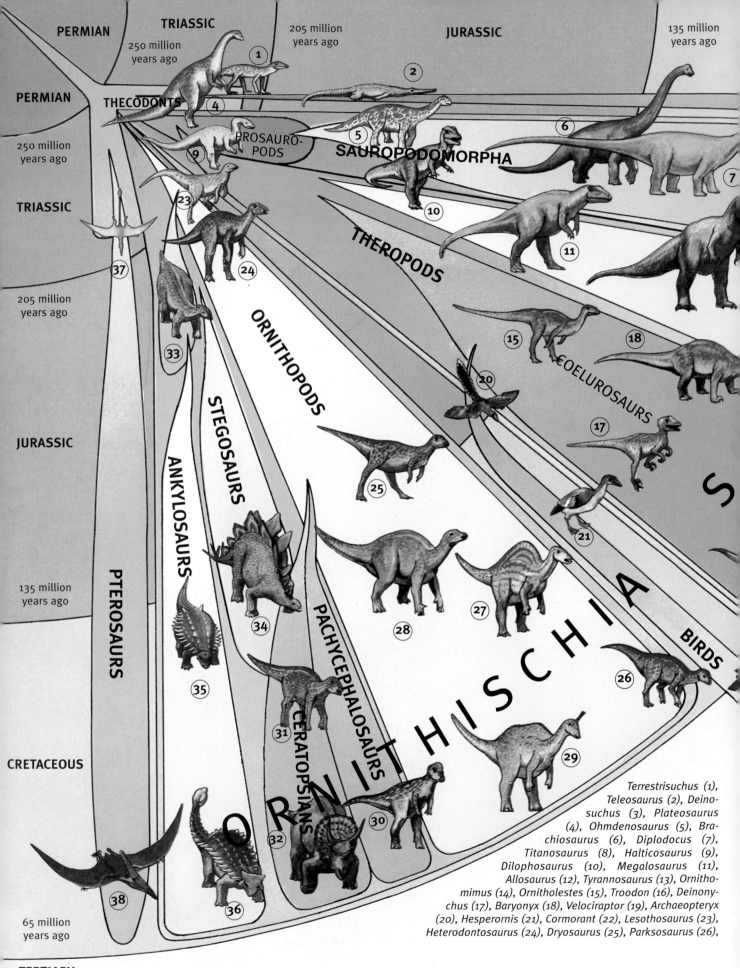

PERMIAN

TRIASSIC

250 million
years ago

205 million
years ago

JURASSIC

135 million
years ago

PERMIAN

250 million
years ago

TRIASSIC

205 million
years ago

JURASSIC

135 million
years ago

CRETACEOUS

65 million
years ago

TERTIARY

THECODONTS

PROSAURO-
PODS

SAUROPODOMORPHA

THEROPODS

COELUROSAURS

ORNITHOPODS

STEGOSAURS

ANKYLOSAURS

PTEROSAURS

PACHYCEPHALOSAURS

CERATOPSIANS

ORNITHISCHIA

BIRDS

*Terrestrisuchus (1),
Teleosaurus (2), Deino-
suchus (3), Plateosaurus
(4), Ohmdenosaurus (5), Brachiosaurus (6), Diplodocus (7),
Titanosaurus (8), Halticosaurus (9),
Dilophosaurus (10), Megalosaurus (11),
Allosaurus (12), Tyrannosaurus (13), Ornithomimus (14), Ornitholestes (15), Troodon (16), Deinonychus (17), Baryonyx (18), Velociraptor (19), Archaeopteryx
(20), Hesperornis (21), Cormorant (22), Lesothosaurus (23),
Heterodontosaurus (24), Dryosaurus (25), Parksosaurus (26),*

10

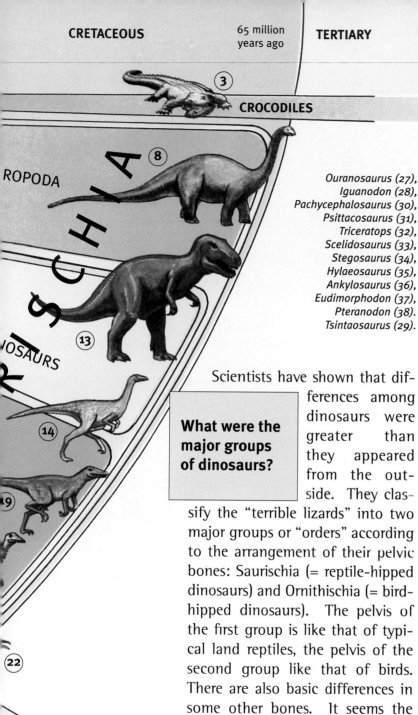

CROCODILES

ROPODA

③

⑧

RISCHIA

⑬

OSAURS

⑭

⑲

㉒

Ouranosaurus (27),
Iguanodon (28),
Pachycephalosaurus (30),
Psittacosaurus (31),
Triceratops (32),
Scelidosaurus (33),
Stegosaurus (34),
Hylaeosaurus (35),
Ankylosaurus (36),
Eudimorphodon (37),
Pteranodon (38).
Tsintaosaurus (29).

What were the major groups of dinosaurs?

Scientists have shown that differences among dinosaurs were greater than they appeared from the outside. They classify the "terrible lizards" into two major groups or "orders" according to the arrangement of their pelvic bones: Saurischia (= reptile-hipped dinosaurs) and Ornithischia (= bird-hipped dinosaurs). The pelvis of the first group is like that of typical land reptiles, the pelvis of the second group like that of birds. There are also basic differences in some other bones. It seems the two groups were separate from the beginning of their development.

The first saurischians were carnivores (meat-eaters). They ran on strong hind legs and used their arms to catch their prey. Some of these predatory dinosaurs later evolved into herbivores (plant-eaters). They now needed much larger amounts of food since their plant diet wasn't as rich in nutrients as the meat they had once eaten. Since they didn't have to

hunt anymore, however, they no longer needed to run. As a result their bodies became larger and larger. They again needed all four legs to walk. These herbivores were called sauropods (= reptile-footed dinosaurs). The predatory dinosaurs that ran on two legs were called theropods (= beast-footed dinosaurs).

Judging from the oldest fossil finds, the first ornithischians were all plant-eaters and ran on their hind legs. Their foot structure is like that of birds, which is why they are called ornithopods (ornith from the Greek word for bird, pod from the Greek word for foot). Other kinds of ornithischian dinosaurs later branched off from these first "bird-footed dinosaurs." As long as the species were still small, they had to be able to run fast to escape their enemies. But the bigger the animals became during the course of their evolution, the more they supported their heavy bodies with their short forelegs. They also moved more slowly. The billed dinosaurs like Iguanodon are an example of this type.

Other ornithischians developed a protective suit of armor as protection against carnivores. The stegosaurs, for example, developed spikes and bony plates along their backs and tails. An armor of bony plates covered the ankylosaurs (armored dinosaurs), and a large bony shield and sharp head horns protected the ceratopsians (horned-face dinosaurs). With this protection they no longer needed to run away every time danger approached. These ornithischians could now walk on four legs and move more slowly.

11

Vegetation in the Triassic Period

Vegetation in the Jurassic Period

The age of dinosaurs began in the middle of the Triassic period, 230 million years ago. At that time, all the continents were joined together and formed one big land mass. Because of the hot, dry climate, there were large deserts. In the humid river valleys and along the coast, however, there were ferns and horsetail grass. In forest areas there were tree ferns, conifers, and gingkos. In addition to insects and frogs, the animal kingdom included many early reptiles: cotylosaurs or "stem-reptiles," rhynchocephalians, turtles, flying reptiles,

When did the first dinosaurs live?

and reptiles resembling lizards, crocodiles, and mammals. It also included the first dinosaurs.

During the **Jurassic period**, 210 to 135 million years ago, the continents gradually began to drift apart. Warm, shallow seas filled the areas between the continents, and the climate became hot and humid. Lush vegetation, especially forests with a variety of trees, covered broad sections of the land. These conditions were favorable for life and dinosaurs flourished. Many new species came into existence and spread across the entire earth. Life on land was no longer characterized by all kinds of reptiles but primarily by dinosaurs.

MEDIUM-SIZED THEROPODS (= "beast-footed" predatory dinosaurs) such as Halticosaurus and Coelophysis were the first dinosaurs in the Triassic Period. Soon larger plant-eaters developed, walking more and more on all four legs. These were the prosauropods — like Plateosaurus. And finally, toward the end of the Triassic period, the first small herbivores running on two legs appeared — ornithopods such as Lesothosaurus.

In the Jurassic Period, many new species came into existence and spread out across the

Vegetation in the Lower Cretaceous Period

Vegetation at the end of the Cretaceous Period

entire earth. The plant-eating sauropods evolved into the largest land animals that ever lived. Whether Brachiosaurus or Apatosaurus, Diplodocus or Seismosaurus, they all lived during the late Jurassic period. Small gazelle- and large billed-dinosaurs grazed in groups. The odd-looking stegosaurs appeared. Along with the smaller, nimble predatory dinosaurs like Compsognathus and Archaeopteryx, there were also giant predators like Allosaurus and Ceratosaurus. They could overpower even giant plant-eaters with their powerful jaws.

When did the last dinosaurs live?

During the **Cretaceous period**, 135 to 65 million years ago, the continents moved further apart, the seas between them became wider and deeper, and the climate became cooler. This led to constantly changing landscapes with more diverse vegetation. Flowering plants evolved, including deciduous trees such as magnolias and plane trees.

The world of dinosaurs also changed several times. Sauropods became increasingly rare. Only a few species survived and continued to evolve. The stegosaurs became entirely extinct. In their place the ankylosaurs appeared, and later the ceratopsians. A large variety of duck-billed dinosaurs also evolved.

The wide variety of animals provided plenty of food for giant carnivores such as Tyrannosaurus. Among the smaller carnivores were many specialized species. There were hunters with huge claws on their hands and feet, ostrich-like hunters with hands that could grip, and toothless egg thieves.

The end of the Cretaceous period brought about such drastic changes everywhere on earth that all dinosaur species gradually became extinct.

Giant Plant-Eating Dinosaurs

Was Plateosaurus the first giant plant-eater?

Scientists have found many complete skeletons of Plateosaurus ("flat lizard") in Germany. Plateosaurus grew up to 25 feet long. It was probably the biggest and one of the most common dinosaurs in its time — the late Triassic period. Plateosaurus looked like a dangerous predator, since it had large claws on its hands. It was actually

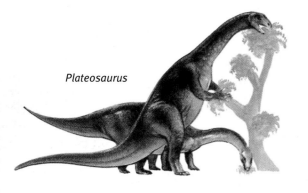

Plateosaurus

a slow-moving plant-eater with small teeth. It only used its claws to protect itself. It is a typical representative of the long-necked prosauropods. These small meat-eating dinosaurs walked on two legs. As they evolved into larger and larger plant-eaters they began to walk more and more on four legs. Scientists think that the prosauropods are the ancestors of the giant dinosaurs, the sauropods.

What are the typical features of sauropods?

Sauropods are the largest animals that ever roamed the earth. They were 10 to 20 times as heavy as an elephant, the biggest land animal today! Only blue whales grow to be as big and heavy as these giant dinosaurs. With such a large body, sauropods needed all four legs and massive bones to be able to walk on land. The trunk-like shape of their legs — especially their forelegs — and the bonding of all five fingers into a column-shaped foot reminds us of elephant legs. The scientific name "sauropod" means "reptile foot."

THE LONG NECK is another unique feature of the giant sauropods and can be half as long as the whole animal. It looks like the arm of a crane and can be lifted high up and can swing to either the side. Although its skeleton was very strong, it was also very lightly built.

Seismosaurus

Mamenchisaurus

Dicraeosaurus

DIPLODOCUS is the longest complete dinosaur ever found. Supersaurus and Seismosaurus (= earthquake lizard) were similar to it, however, and could have been 300 to 400 feet long. We don't really know though, since so far scientists have found only one bone from each of them.

Saltasaurus

What differences were there between the sauropods?

Brachiosaurus (= arm lizard) was the largest and heaviest of the giant sauropods. It weighed more than 80 tons and stood out from all the others. Since it had such long forelegs, the line of its back sloped noticeably downward, ending with its short tail. Its head, which had a very powerful set of teeth, towered up to 35 or even 50 feet high on a very long neck. Only Ultrasaurus could have been similarly large or even larger, but our knowledge of that dinosaur is still incomplete. All other species had much shorter forelegs.

Camarasaurus (= room lizard) had a much shorter neck in comparison to Brachiosaurus. Its body, head, and teeth, however, were similarly thickset and strong.

Dicraeosaurus (= forked lizard) also had a short neck, but was much slimmer.

Most other species had long necks. Mamenchisaurus (= lizard from Mamenchi) and Barosaurus (= heavy lizard) had the longest necks, almost 30 feet long. Diplodocus (= double beam) had the longest tail, about 49 feet long. This made it the longest complete dinosaur ever found — measuring 89 feet in all. It was also the slimmest, weighing only about 10 tons.

Camarasaurus

Apatosaurus

Diplodocus

Brachiosaurus

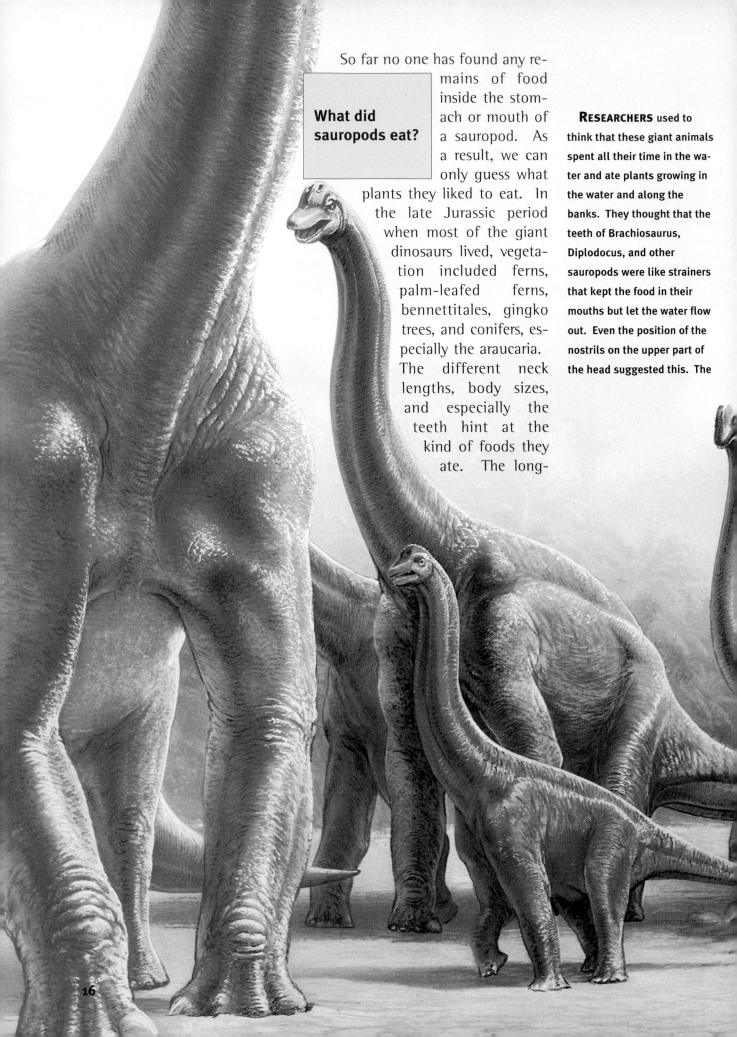

What did sauropods eat?

So far no one has found any remains of food inside the stomach or mouth of a sauropod. As a result, we can only guess what plants they liked to eat. In the late Jurassic period when most of the giant dinosaurs lived, vegetation included ferns, palm-leafed ferns, bennettitales, gingko trees, and conifers, especially the araucaria. The different neck lengths, body sizes, and especially the teeth hint at the kind of foods they ate. The long-

RESEARCHERS used to think that these giant animals spent all their time in the water and ate plants growing in the water and along the banks. They thought that the teeth of Brachiosaurus, Diplodocus, and other sauropods were like strainers that kept the food in their mouths but let the water flow out. Even the position of the nostrils on the upper part of the head suggested this. The giant sauropods could have rested in the water and breathed without raising their heads — just like crocodiles or hippopotamuses. They would have only gone on land on rare occasions — to lay eggs, for example. Today, however, we are certain that the giant dinosaurs could walk well and usually looked for food on land.

necked species such as Brachiosaurus, for example, could reach the treetops. Lighter species like Diplodocus even stood on their hind legs to do this. Diplodocus, however, could only strip off leaves from the branches and fronds with its thin, pin-shaped teeth. Camarasaurus, on the other hand, could bite off complete bunches of leaves and shoots. Since their teeth were not suitable for chewing, giant dinosaurs swallowed golfball- to baseball-sized stones and the plant parts were ground between them as they rubbed together in their stomachs.

Given their small heads and the simple set of teeth, it is amazing that they were able to supply their giant bodies with enough food. The animals must have spent most of the day feeding. Some scientists think it is possible that sauropods — with their enormous

food needs and their ability to eat away the tops of trees — were partly responsible for the drastic changes in the plant world in their era.

We can conclude from footprints that a few sauropod species lived in herds. This makes sense, especially for the protection of their young, since there were also large predators at that time such as the carnosaurs Allosaurus, Ceratosaurus, and Megalosaurus. A sauropod had nothing for protection besides its long tail, which it could use like a whip. We know this because scientists have found tailbones that show signs of healed injuries that probably were caused by such blows. A predatory dinosaur had to be careful not to be within striking distance of the whip-like tail of a sauropod.

Did the giant sauropods have enemies?

One of the enemies of Brachiosaurus was the predatory dinosaur Ceratosaurus.

Terrifying Predatory Dinosaurs

<table>
<tr><td>

Which predatory dinosaurs were the biggest?

</td></tr>
</table>

Among the first English dinosaur finds, there was a fragment of a lower jaw with only a few teeth. Since it was apparently from a huge carnivorous lizard, its discoverer gave it the name Megalosaurus (= giant lizard). Because the other body parts were missing, he didn't know exactly what it looked like or how big it was. Consequently, he assumed that it walked on four legs (see p. 5).

Since then many new finds have been made, but still no complete skeleton. Only by comparing the finds with bones of other giant predators (carnosaurs) were scientists finally able to conclude that Megalosaurus walked on its hind legs like other carnosaurs. It was probably up to 30 feet long, and weighed as much as one ton.

We have been able to make a much more reliable picture of Allosaurus (= different kind of lizard). Scientists have found more than 60 skeletons in quarries in Utah. Allosaurus was from 35 to 40 feet long and weighed one to two tons. Plant-eaters were certainly part of its diet — scientists found a tail segment from Apatosaurus with deep teeth marks and broken bits of Allosaurus teeth embedded in it.

Two other species that lived 80 million years later in the Cretaceous period must have been even bigger: Tyrannosaurus (= tyrant lizard) in North America and Tarbosaurus (= frightening lizard) in Mongolia. Although the skeletons are incomplete — usually the tail is missing — their length is estimated at 45 to 50 feet, their height at 20 feet, and their body weight at five to six tons. The heads were massive. The skull of Tarbosaurus is 4.75 feet long, that of Tyrannosaurus 4.5 feet. Their dagger-like teeth were 6 inches long and so strong they could even hold on to large, fiercely struggling prey. We do not know, however, whether these giants could really run after their prey or if they were slow-moving. They may have lived on carrion (dead animals) or on animals that smaller predators had killed. They could easily have driven the smaller dinosaurs away from their prey. The arms of Tyrannosaurus were strangely short and weak, and their hands only had two fingers. In contrast, Therizinosaurus (= sickle lizard) had a giant claw 2.6 feet long! We don't know if this was its only claw or even how big the whole animal was.

SPINOSAURUS

(= spiked lizard) must have been a very impressive predator as well. It was up to 40 feet long and had a six-foot high skin "sail" spanning its back. Did it use this impressive "sail" to intimidate rivals and competitors, or was it used to regulate body temperature — absorbing heat from the sun when it was cold and giving off body heat to help it cool down when it was hot?

Reconstruction of the head of an

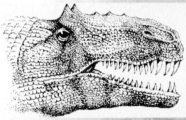

Allosaurus

Dilophosaurus

Tyrannosaurus attacks a herd of Triceratops.

Rohebook 95

19

In addition to the giant carnivorous dinosaurs — the carnosaurs —

How did small predatory dinosaurs hunt?

other smaller and slimmer species of predatory dinosaurs evolved — the coelurosaurs. This name means "hollow-boned lizard" and refers to the light bone structure of the dinosaurs in this group or suborder. They also ran on long hind legs, but were twice as fast as their larger relatives and could run at speeds of 20 to 25 miles per hour. The body and tail of these dinosaurs formed a straight, horizontal line, and their necks were held up in an S shape. They had more slender heads than their giant relations and had jaws with many narrow, sharp teeth. Their arms were only half as long as their legs, and the sharp claws on their hands were very effective for clutching their prey. Coelurosaurs hunted small animals such as insects and lizards and sometimes even a young animal of their own species. They might even have taken a piece of meat from the prey of larger meat-eating dinosaurs. Many species of these small predatory dinosaurs already lived during the Triassic period, for example the 16-foot long Halticosaurus (= nimble lizard).

Later, during the Jurassic period, there were species that were even more slender, and had even longer arms and longer tails. The backs of their tails had stiffened to become a kind of balancing rod in most cases. The extremely agile Ornitholestes (= bird robber), excavated in North America, was 6.5 feet long. Compsognathus (= pretty jaw) was the smallest, about the size of a chicken.

In 1860 researchers made a sen-

Was the prehistoric bird a small predatory dinosaur?

sational find in southern Germany. An imprint of a typical bird feather was found in a layer of limestone from the Jurassic period. This indicated that birds existed already at the same time as the largest and smallest dinosaurs, in the middle of the Mesozoic era! Shortly after this, two more complete skeletons were found with clear impressions of complete plumage and feathered wings. The asymmetrical shape of the individ-

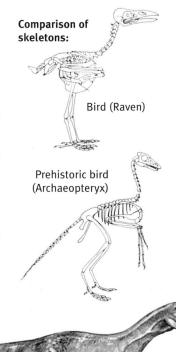

Comparison of skeletons:

Bird (Raven)

Prehistoric bird (Archaeopteryx)

Small predatory dinosaur (Compsognathus)

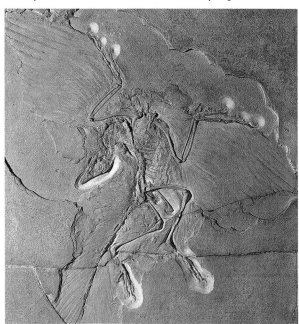

Skeleton and feather impressions of the prehistoric bird Archaeopteryx. This limestone slab was found in Solnhofen, Germany.

Archaeopteryx, the predatory dinosaur Compsognathus (left), and three pterosaurs (right)

ARCHAEOPTERYX,

the prehistoric bird, is an intermediate step in the evolution of a predatory dinosaur into a bird. It could run, climb and fly. It probably did more gliding than flying, but it certainly could have flown upwards for short stretches by flapping its wings vigorously. It preyed on insects and small lizards.

ual feathers and their arrangement on the wing are exactly the same as on birds today. This is clear evidence that Archaeopteryx (= ancient wings) could fly.

Archaeopteryx's skeleton does not look at all like that of a bird, however. There is a long tail like that of a dinosaur — birds have a short rump. There are real teeth in the jaw whereas a bird has a toothless beak. There are three clawed fingers that jut out from the front edge of the wings. There are also ribs on its lower neck, ribs around the abdomen, and individual pelvic bones — all the same as small predatory dinosaurs had. On the other hand there is no massive breastbone, no stiffened backbone, and no large pelvis as with birds! Only a few bones and joints have shapes like those of a bird. If it were not for the feathers, the find would have been classified as a small

predatory dinosaur due to the bone structure. This is actually what happened with two earlier fossil finds. It wasn't until much later that researchers recognized that they were Archaeopteryx specimens.

This prehistoric bird is undoubtedly an intermediate stage in the gradual evolution of a hollowboned dinosaur (coelurosaur) into a typical bird. In the course of its evolution there were no great leaps or stages. If there were, it would be easy for us to say it was clearly a saurian or reptile up to this point, but from there on it was clearly a bird. The individual body parts did not change all at once, but only slowly, one after another. As a result, Archaeopteryx had a mixture of features: feathers and wings clearly show early bird characteristics, but the teeth and the tail still show reptilian characteristics.

Both the eyes and the brain of this bird-like, six-foot-long reptile were unusually large, like those of an eagle or owl. Since their eyes pointed forward — most dinosaurs had eyes pointing to the sides — Saurornithoides (= bird-like lizard) could locate and home in on their prey with great accuracy. They could probably do so even during twilight hours or at night. They were agile even when tracking and hunting nocturnal, mouse-like mammals. If fleeing animals hid, this dinosaur could use its long arms to fish them out of dense undergrowth or even out of cracks between rocks. Saurornithoides needed an efficient brain to be able to use such sophisticated hunting methods. Some researchers assume that Saurornithoides even looked like a bird — it may have been covered with feathers.

Why did Saurornithoides have such large eyes?

Except for their long arms and tails, the figures of these slim, long-legged predators looked so much like ostriches and emus that the scientists named them after these birds. Ornithomimus means "bird-imitator"; Struthiomimus means "ostrich-imitator"; Dromiceiomimus means "emu-imitator"; and Gallimimus means "chicken-imitator." They could run as fast as present-day ostriches. They were faster than any other dinosaur and could probably run at speeds of more than 30 miles per hour. They probably had a beak like that of a bird — we know they did not have teeth — but we do not know whether they also ate the same diet as birds.

What do we know about "ostrich" dinosaurs?

THERE ARE many unanswered questions about the "ostrich dinosaurs." Did they live on insects and lizards, or eat shrimp and snails? Did they use their hands to dig up eggs laid by other dinosaurs? Or were they plant-eaters that used their hands to pick leaves and shoots, fruits and seeds? Did they grip the food with their hands or with their beaks? We also do not know whether they lived in herds or whether they cared for their young. It is even possible that they bore live young. The large opening in the pelvic bone suggests this might have been the case.

Saurornithoides, a bird-like dinosaur with big eyes

Ornithomimus (= bird imitator), an "ostrich" dinosaur

The egg thief
Oviraptor

*Velociraptor fighting
Protoceratops*

VELOCIRAPTOR
must have been a dangerous hunter — thanks to its long legs it could catch up with any animal that tried to flee. Thirty sharp teeth, clawed hands for gripping, and sickle-shaped shredding claws on its feet made it a terrifying predator.

What did Oviraptor eat?

In 1922 paleontologists discovered a fossil site that looked almost like a crime scene. Hidden under the sand, they found the crushed skull of a small predatory dinosaur on top of a nest that had probably belonged to the horned dinosaur Protoceratops. Did an alert female surprise and kill an oviraptor at work? The thief's unusually short and strong jaws, which had only a single tooth, were particularly suitable for opening the thick-skinned shells of dinosaur eggs. That is why this six-foot-long predator was called Oviraptor meaning "egg thief" or "egg taker" in Latin. Other species may have eaten snails or other animals with shells.

Did predators always win their battles?

One of the most interesting and exciting dinosaur finds was made in Mongolia in 1971. Researchers excavated complete skeletons of a predator and its plant-eating victim. The roughly six-foot-long carnivore Velociraptor (= rapid thief) had attacked a Protoceratops of about the same size and was seriously injured during the struggle. Both animals died with their teeth and claws still buried in their opponent.

*A group of Deinonychus ambush
a duck-billed dinosaur, Tenontosaurus.*

In 1963 another unusual predatory dinosaur was found in Montana, in layers of stone dating from the early Cretaceous period.

**How did
"terrible claw"
hunt?**

It was no giant — only about five feet tall when standing upright, and 9 to 12 feet long. More than half its length was its tail. This tail was stiffened and was used for balancing — like the tail of a kangaroo. Its teeth and clawed hands and feet must have made it a dangerous hunter.

On each foot there was a particularly large and curved claw. Deinonychus kept it folded up while walking, but when it jumped on its prey this claw could be snapped forward and plunged into the victim's body with a strong kick. This is why scientists named this carnivore "terrible claw" (Deinonychus). A blow with this claw was made even more effective when Deinonychus grabbed its prey with its hands and sank its teeth into the flesh of its prey. The victim could not even free itself by violently twisting its body, since the teeth of Deinonychus angled backwards in its mouth and only dug in deeper when its prey struggled.

This hunting style of Deinonychus is similar to that of present-day leopards, which are similar in size and can also defeat animals larger than themselves. The discovery of bones from several of these animals at one site is evidence for the theory that they hunted in packs. The unusually large brain cavity indicates that Deinonychus was capable of complicated modes of behavior and may have lived in communities.

THE PREY OF DEINONY-CHUS were probably mostly young animals of other species of dinosaurs — most often the young of the herbivores Hypsilophodon and Iguanodon.

WHAT DID BARYONYX
feed on? The long jaw full of
sharp, pointed teeth, and the
fact that scientists found fish
scales in the stomach region
of the fossilized skeleton suggest it ate fish. Did Baryonyx
sit near or in the water and
toss fish onto the shore with
its large claw? Or did it eat
carrion (dead animals)? The
claw could have been used to
slit open the carcass so that
its long snout could reach the
meat inside.

*Did Baryonyx eat fish or
carrion?*

What was the giant with the "terrible hand"?

At a dig in Mongolia, re-searchers found the arm and shoulder bones of an unknown species of dino-saur. The arms were 8 feet long! Unfortunately no other bones were found. Sci-entists still do not know what this enormous predator looked like. Its eight-foot-long arms were almost as long as a whole Deinonychus and four times as long as an arm of Deinonychus! On each hand there were gigantic claws that could have stabbed and torn into even very large animals. Re-searchers were so impressed that they called the new species Deinocheirus, or "terrible hand."

If we compare the arm bones of Deinocheirus with those of ostrich-like dinosaurs, whose arms were similarly constructed but only about one fourth as long, then Deinocheirus must have been fifty percent larger than Tyrannosaurus!

Dinosaur enthusiasts and re-searchers all over the world anx-iously await more finds that could shed new light on this giant with the "terrible hand."

How was Baryonyx discovered?

In 1986 an amateur collector found the claw of an entirely new type of predator in a clay pit in Sur-rey, England. Researchers later found more of the skeleton. It was over 24 feet long and had a crocodile-like head about three feet long — and twice as many teeth as most carnivores. Its front legs were very long and strong — scientists think it proba-bly walked on all fours, which was very unusual for a predator!

A large claw, over a foot long, gave this dinosaur its name: Bary-onyx or "heavy claw." The claw was probably located on the hand, though scientists are still not sure of this.

The Curious Bird-Footed Dinosaurs

How large were ornithopods?

All of the species belonging to the second main category or order of dinosaurs — Ornithischia ("Ornithischia" means "bird-hipped") — were plant-eaters. The first ornithischians lived in the Triassic period. As with the other major group — Saurischia — the first known species were quite small and could easily run on two legs. They looked a lot like small predatory dinosaurs, but in several details their body structure was fundamentally different. The bone structure of their feet was more like that of birds, which is why these early ornithischians are called ornithopods — "bird-footed" dinosaurs. They did have the typical plant-eater's jaw with angular, closely-packed teeth for ripping and chewing. The tip of the jaw, however, had no teeth, since a horn beak overlapped the jawbone.

In later periods some ornithopods evolved into 37-foot-long monsters weighing up to five tons — Iguanodon, for example. The early species, however, were small and light — between three and seven feet long. Among these was Lesothosaurus. It had four toes on each of its long legs and five fingers on each hand. It used its hands to support itself and to scrape up food. Lesothosaurus tore off leaves, shoots, and buds with its beak and then thoroughly chewed and ground them before swallowing. If it met a predator its only defense was to run.

Soon new and larger species developed. They stood out because of the noticeably longer canine teeth, particularly in males. It isn't likely that these teeth were used against predatory dinosaurs, however. Instead they were probably used during fights between rivals. The members of this group were called heterodontosaurs (= different-toothed lizards).

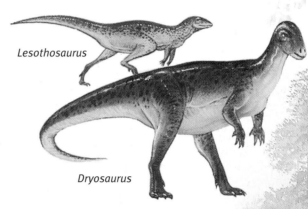

Lesothosaurus

Dryosaurus

How fast were "gazelle" dinosaurs?

Gazelle dinosaurs were among the fastest of all dinosaurs. Scientists think they probably reached speeds of up to 30 miles per hour with their long legs. This type of plant-eater seems to have adapted successfully in nearly every situation — species from this group existed throughout most of the Mesozoic era. They were between 3 and 12 feet long and occupied a similar position in nature as today's medium-sized herbivores — gazelles, antelope, deer, and kangaroos. Like these animals they lived mostly in herds.

The five- to eight-foot-long Hypsilophodon (= ridged teeth) is

DRYOSAURUS

(= oak lizard) was the largest hypsilophodon or "gazelle" species. It was more than 12 feet long. Nanosaurus (= dwarf lizard), on the other hand, only grew to a length of three feet.

CAMPTOSAURUS

(= bent lizard — because of the curved upper thigh bone) and Tenontosaurus (= tendon lizard — after the conspicuous bony tendons that ran along the spinal column reinforced the back) were also widespread. Ouranosaurus (= varanus lizard — from Arabic waran: monitor lizard) had long extensions on their vertebrae. It is still not clear whether they supported a "sail" of skin or a camel-like hump.

representative of the whole family of gazelle or hypsilophodon dinosaurs and roamed Europe and North America during the early Cretaceous period.

The largest ornithopods — up to 37 feet long — are sometimes called billed dinosaurs and had snouts tipped with a beak-like horny covering. This beak was apparently very good for shredding plants. It grew continuously and sharpened itself when used. The teeth were arranged in tight rows and formed a continuous grinding surface, which ensured that food was well chewed.

The most common and best-known member of this family was Iguanodon (= iguana tooth, see p. 5). Iguanodon is also representative of this type of dinosaur. Remains of Iguanodon have been discovered in Europe, Asia, and North America. In its day, Iguanodon played a similar role in nature to that of the present-day zebra and antelope. Judging by the numerous footprints that have been preserved, researchers are fairly certain that these dinosaurs lived in small groups or herds. In this way their young were better protected against predators. Iguanodon could probably fight back if attacked, since it had a sharp, dagger-like thumbnail that it could use as a weapon. Timely retreat, however, was a safer defense, and at such times these animals — weighing up to 5 tons — could even run on their two hind legs. They used all four legs when walking normally and so the three middle fingers each ended in a small hoof instead of the usual claw.

> **Which is the best known billed dinosaur?**

The Iguanodon (left) and the gazelle-like dinosaur Hypsilophodon (below)

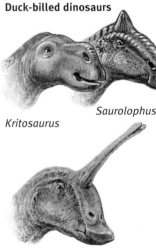

Most of the more than twenty duck-billed dinosaurs (hadrosaurs) can easily be distinguished from each other by the unusual bone structures on their heads. Otherwise they all look very similar. Their beaks and teeth are more specialized than those of their ancestors, the billed dinosaurs. Each had more than 1,000 small, ridged teeth, which were grouped tightly together into grinding or chewing surfaces. A large tongue pressed the plant material between the batteries to make chewing easier. Cheeks and pouches enclosed the mouth area.

The beaks of the various species varied greatly in shape and were apparently adapted to the type of food each species preferred. They can only be roughly compared with ducks' bills in terms of width. Otherwise they were harder and rather short, and there were teeth in the jaws behind them. Furthermore, they were not used in water but for biting and tearing off vegetation on land.

The significance of the strange structures on their heads is still a puzzle. Some believe that they were used as snorkels, others say that they were cooling mechanisms or important for producing sound or as marks by which animals of the same species could recognize each other. Since it was only on males that these structures were very large and probably brightly colored as well — whereas on females they were smaller or even nonexistent — they can hardly have been of vital importance. They probably played an important role in communication between animals of the same species, for example in fights between rivals — just like the antlers, horns, inflated throat sacs, or colored combs on the heads of present-day animals.

All these possibilities suggest that duck-billed dinosaurs must have been very sociable animals with a clear hierarchy in their herds. Young animals had a special position and tagged along behind the adults when the herd moved on. In excavations scientists have found that females laid their eggs in colonies of nests, and that the young animals remained in the nest, protected by their mother, for a long time after hatching out of their eggs.

Duck-billed dinosaurs

Kritosaurus

Saurolophus

Tsintaosaurus

A group of Corythosaurus

Pachycephalosaurs ("dome-headed" dinosaurs) displaying rivalry

Dome-headed dinosaurs

Stego-ceras

Prenocephale

Homalocephale

Which dinosaur had the thickest skull?

A rather strange group or sub-order of ornithischians are the pachycephalosaurs (= thick-headed dinosaurs), also called "dome-headed" dinosaurs. The name says it all: the bones of the upper skull were enormously reinforced and up to 10 inches thick in the largest species. Apparently this skull was used as a battering ram when animals of the same species battled for rank. The pachycephalosaurs fought for the top position in the herd in the same way that present-day wild rams do. They charged each other at a speed of about 20 miles per hour. The spine was also sturdier and stiffer than usual to prevent the force of the impact from damaging the back or neck.

All this is the result of guess-work, however, as little of these animals has been preserved — almost nothing but skulls of males. Pachycephalosaurus had a skull over 24 inches long. Scientists estimate that its body was about 18 feet long. Other species were much smaller. Homalocephalus (= regular head) reached a length of 9 feet. One type of micropachycephalosaur (= small dome-headed dinosaur) was about the size of a chicken, 20 inches long.

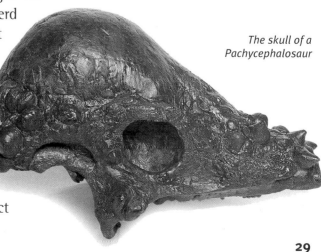

The skull of a Pachycephalosaur

Horns, Spines, and Armor

In 1922 scientists working in Mongolia found skeletons of dinosaurs that were as much as six feet long.

What was the parrot-like beak for?

The skeletons were found in layers of rock dating from the early Cretaceous period. Because of their parrot-like beaks and the unusual shape of their heads they called this species Psittacosaurus (= parrot lizard). The short yet strong beak was pointed and sharp-edged. With this beak they could bite off or split open even very tough parts of plants. Their bite must

Psittacosaurus or "parrot-beak" dinosaurs

have been extremely powerful, since the skull has many attachment points for large, powerful muscles — especially on a high ridge at the back of the head. Because of their distinctive characteristics, researchers find it easy to identify even very small skeletons of this type. In most cases it is very hard to match skeletons of young animals with those of adult dinosaurs. The smallest "chicks" were 10 to 11 inches long with skulls less than 1.5 inches long. Naturally, the heads and beaks of the young were more rounded and

not as strong. Of course these tender young animals were easy prey for small predatory dinosaurs. For this reason researchers assumed that Psittacosaurus mothers looked after their babies for a relatively long time. Their mothers may also have fed them a paste of mashed leaves.

This 6-foot-long dinosaur was only 30 inches tall, but it weighed up to two tons. Scientists know

How did Protoceratops defend itself?

quite a bit about this species. Not only have they found more than 100 skeletons of all sizes in Mongolia, but eggs and nests as well. The name Protoceratops means "ancestor of the horned-face dinosaur" (ceratopsia). Protoceratops did not yet have long, sharp horns on its head, but only armored knobs. Like the later ceratopsians, however, Protoceratops walked on all fours and had a horny beak on its snout and a bony shield extending from the back of its head. This shield covered the neck and probably served several functions. It was an attachment point for the powerful jaw muscles and it also provided protection for the neck, which could easily be injured by predators. It was also used to threaten or impress. Since the animals lived in groups there would certainly have been rivalries and struggles over feeding and nesting places. It would not have been safe to rely solely on the strong, sharp beak.

PROTOCERATOPS had a strong, sharp beak. The skeletons of two dead predators — Velociraptor and Oviraptor — prove just how effective a weapon this beak was. In one case Velociraptor attacked a plant-eater, Protoceratops, that obviously put up quite a fight. While the predator held the prey's head firmly and tried to kill it, the wounded Protoceratops was still able to fatally wound its attacker with its sharp beak. Both animals died while locked in this position and were covered over by sand.

ALL CERATOPSIANS
(= horn-faced dinosaurs) had large heads with horns and a bony shield or "frill." The frills of Torosaurus (= bull lizard) and Pentaceratops (= five-horn face) stretched over half the length of their backs! Most species of horn-faced dinosaurs had a short frill, however. Long-frilled types usually had long eyebrow horns and a short nose horn. Short-frilled types had a long nose horn and short eyebrow horns. Monoclonius (= single horn) had a nose horn over 28 inches long! The largest and best known species belong to the genus Triceratops (= three-horn face). Their eyebrow horns were up to 3 feet long and came to a very sharp point.

How many horns did the horned dinosaurs have?

The "real" ceratopsians appeared in the final tenth of the age of dinosaurs, in other words about 80 million years ago. Their well-preserved and numerous remains have only been found in North America. Scientists have found over 100 skulls from Triceratops (= three-horn face) alone. The ceratopsians were all giants. They were over 16 feet long and had horns, a strong "parrot" beak, and a large head with a bony shield or "frill" extending back behind the head. The beak and the sharp grinding teeth could handle tough leaves and twigs or other solid vegetation. The beak could also be used against aggressors, however, and was just as effective against enemies as the horns or the frill at the back of the head.

Most or perhaps even all of the species in this suborder lived in herds. Since they lived in a time when huge carnivores like Tyrannosaurus were alive, it makes sense that they would have lived in groups. They could then form a defensive circle in order to protect themselves and their young. There were two types of ceratopsians: ones with long head-frills and ones with short head-frills.

"Horn-faced" dinosaurs

Protocer-
atops

Lepto-
ceratops

Chasmosaurus

Styraco-
saurus

Triceratops

Arrhinoceratops

*Pentaceratops,
the "five-horned face"*

31

The stegosaurs (= plated dino- saurs) were also herbivores and walked on all fours, but they had a different method for scaring away their enemies. A double row of bony spines and plates extended from the neck and across the back to the end of the tail. These plates were only loosely fixed in the skin. Stegosaurs may have been able to aim the pointed spines in the direction of an enemy. The plates, however, were unsuitable for active defense since they were made of light, porous bone. They were probably well supplied with blood vessels and covered with a thin layer of skin. This would have helped stegosaurs to control their body temperature. The spikes at the end of the tails, however, would have been effective weapons. An attacker would have to watch out if a stegosaur swung its tail.

It is still unclear whether these plates were located opposite one another along the spine or in an alternating, staggered pattern. In the first finds in North America the plates were lying scattered among the other bones. This is why scientists first thought the plates lay flat against

> **How did plated dinosaurs protect themselves?**

the back on both sides — like roof-tiles. This is how they got the name Stegosaurus (= roof lizard).

In proportion to their body size the stegosaurs had a very small head. Their beaked mouth and minute teeth were suitable only for eating soft vegetation.

Stegosaurus, found only in North America, was the largest stegosaur. It was about 24 feet long and weighed up to two tons. At the tip of the tail it had two pairs of spikes. 30-inch-high plates ran along the rest of the back. Along the back of Kentrosaurus (= spiny-tailed lizard) there was a gradual change from plates at the front to spikes at the tail. Dacentrurus (= spiny tail), found at several sites in Europe, had only spikes.

Allosaurus

Stegosaurus

Kentrosaurus

Brachiosaurus

Dicraeosaurus

Pterodactylus

Dryosaurus

Rhamphorhynchus

Kentrosaurus

Plated dinosaurs

Huayango-saurus

Chialingosaurus

Tuojiangosaurus

Compsognathus

33

Were armored dinosaurs invulnerable?

The armored dinosaurs or anky-losaurs first appeared during the Cretaceous period. They were even better equipped than the Jurassic stegosaurs to withstand attack. These stocky plant-eaters walked on all fours and were covered from head to tail with a rugged armor of bony plates beneath a tough, leathery skin. Most species had a row of sturdy spikes or spines on the sides of their bodies and tails. The tails of some species terminated in a giant, bony club, which they could use as a striking weapon. When these animals were threatened by predators they probably pressed themselves to the ground and relied on their impregnable armor. If an attacker was able to get hold of the unprotected belly, however, it was all over for the herbivore. We know of more than 30 species of ankylosaurs, most of which lived towards the end of the Cretaceous period. One ancestor, however, Scelidosaurus (= jointed lizard), lived more than 100 million years earlier. Its armor consisted of bony plates and spines arranged in seven rows along its body.

Scelidosaurus

Pointed-tailed armored dinosaurs

Nodosaurus

Hylaeosaurus

Silvisaurus

Sauropelta

Struthiosaurus

Panoplosaurus

Armored skin of the ankylosaur Euoplocephalus cutleri

Euoplocephalus

Club-tailed armored dinosaurs

Talarurus

Saichania

Pinacosaurus

Ankylosaurus using its clubbed tail to drive off Tyrannosaurus

Later armored dinosaurs belonged to one of two groups. The first group were the slender nodosaurs (= knotted lizards), with pointed tails, narrow heads, and loose armor. The second group were the stocky ankylosaurs (= crooked lizards), with wider heads and a club-like tail.

The first group had skin that appeared to be studded with large lumps. Sauropelta (= lizard shield) was especially large, weighing three tons and having a length of 23 feet. Later, at the end of the age of dinosaurs, Palaeoscincus (= old lizard) also grew to similar size.

Stronger, more complete armor was typical of the second group. 20-foot-long Talarurus from Mongolia had bony plates two inches thick. Here too, the largest species appeared latest: Euoplocephalus (= typical armored head) and Ankylosaurus were both about 30 feet long. Ossified tendons made the rear part of the tail into a rigid clubbed stalk that could make very accurate blows.

35

General Characteristics of Dinosaurs

Skin is one of those parts of the body that cannot usually be fossilized.

What did dinosaur skin look like?

Sometimes, however, scientists find impressions of dinosaur skin. In one such case they found a dinosaur — Anatosaurus (= duck lizard) — that died during a sand storm and was covered by dry sand. It left an impression of its skin in the sand, and the sand turned to rock. The Anatosaurus skin was hairless, dry, and tough and divided into small, raised areas of thicker, hardened skin with folds of softer skin in between. Small bony plates were deposited in the skin beneath the shields of tough skin.

The dinosaurs' ancestors, and their relatives the crocodiles, already had these bony plates. Scientists assume that this type of skin was widespread among the dinosaurs. The armored dinosaurs had the most highly developed bony plates. They were up to two inches thick and lay close together, forming an unbroken layer over the whole upper surface of the body. This gave them a strong but flexible armor. Above this there was a layer of tough, hardened skin. The pattern in the skin corresponded to the mosaic of bony plates underneath it. Where the tough skin thickened over pointed or arched bony plates, it formed thick pointed horns or humps.

Dinosaur skin was probably as varied as that of present-day reptiles. We do not know what colors or patterns dinosaur skin may have had. The skin colors and patterns in pictures of dinosaurs are based on guesswork or pure fantasy!

Over a century ago, the American dinosaur researcher O.C. Marsh first examined a complete skeleton of a large dinosaur.

Did some dinosaurs need two brains?

He noted with surprise: "The small dimensions of the head and brain indicate a slow and stupid reptile ... ." This view was so widely accepted for so long that the term "dinosaur" came to mean someone outdated and dull.

This view is unfair to many species, however, especially the smaller, agile predatory dinosaurs or the sociable, lively duck-billed dinosaurs.

The predatory dinosaur Saurornithoides had a relatively large brain, almost as big as those of mammals or birds. The shape of the cranial cavity in a Saurornithoides skull shows that certain parts of the brain were unusually

THE STRUCTURE of the brain cavity in duck-billed dinosaur skulls indicates that they could also see and hear well and had a good sense of smell. These senses were especially important for defenseless plant-eaters. They needed to be able to sense approaching enemies in time to flee.

Skin impression from a sauropod. The pattern of rigid areas and soft folds of skin is clearly visible.

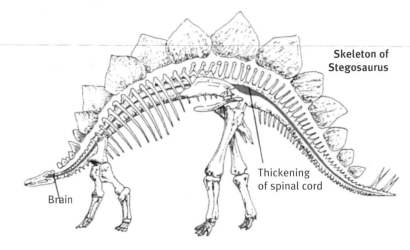

Skeleton of Stegosaurus

Thickening of spinal cord

Brain

Stegosaurus had a very small brain in relation to its body size. The enlargement of the spinal cord is not a second brain, however, but only a nerve relay for controlling the tail muscles.

Only the brain in the skull is the real thing. It obviously met the needs of this well-armed herbivore, since the stegosaurs existed for many millions of years!

well developed. These included the areas responsible for sight and smell and for complicated movements such as balancing or feeling and gripping with its hands.

The ankylosaurs and stegosaurs had the smallest brains in relation to their body size. The brain of elephant-sized Stegosaurus can't have been any bigger than a walnut. Was this big enough? In the hip region of the backbone there was another, larger cavity for a nerve center. Was this enlargement of the spinal cord a second brain, as some have claimed? Certainly not. It was only the normal relay station for the nerve paths in the rear of the body and in the tail. Most vertebrates with long tails have a noticeably thicker spinal cord in this location. And the tail of Stegosaurus wasn't just enormous — as long as the rest of its body — it was also vitally important as a defensive weapon. In order to deliver an accurate blow it needed a nervous system large enough to give it precise control over all its tail muscles.

Did dinosaurs have voices?

There is still no proof that dinosaurs had voices, but there is evidence that suggests they might have. Among today's reptiles crocodiles communicate with each other using a variety of sounds. The male of some species can roar or grunt loudly to intimidate rivals or attract females. Their young can even call from within the egg to tell their mothers they are about to hatch. Why shouldn't their nearest relatives, the dinosaurs, also have had voices?

The bone structures of the skull do not provide a clear answer. Some scientists have wondered if the structure extending from the noses of some duck-billed dinosaurs could have been used to produce or amplify sounds. Some researchers believe this is likely. According to them, Lambeosaurus could have produced trumpet-like sounds. Such sounds might have served as signals to the herd. They might have been used, for example, to warn other animals browsing in the thick vegetation that enemies were coming.

Sound production needs to be accompanied by a suitable receiver, a sensitive faculty for hearing. In the ear of a completely preserved skull researchers did, in fact, find small, fine bones for the transfer of sound. This suggests that the animal had good hearing.

Some scientists think that the structure extending upward from the nose enabled duck-billed dinosaurs to produce sounds.

Parasaurolophus

Lambeosaurus

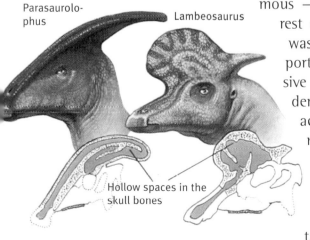

Hollow spaces in the skull bones

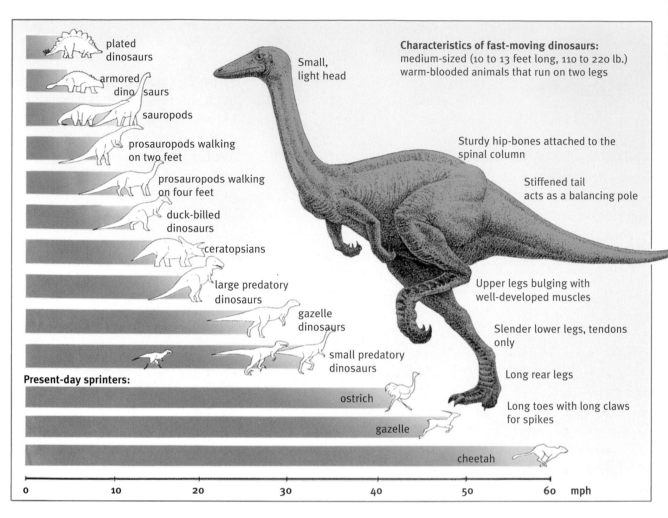

plated
dinosaurs

armored
dino saurs

sauropods

prosauropods walking
on two feet

prosauropods walking
on four feet

duck-billed
dinosaurs

ceratopsians

large predatory
dinosaurs

gazelle
dinosaurs

small predatory
dinosaurs

Present-day sprinters:

ostrich

gazelle

cheetah

Small,
light head

Characteristics of fast-moving dinosaurs:
medium-sized (10 to 13 feet long, 110 to 220 lb.)
warm-blooded animals that run on two legs

Sturdy hip-bones attached to the
spinal column

Stiffened tail
acts as a balancing pole

Upper legs bulging with
well-developed muscles

Slender lower legs, tendons
only

Long rear legs

Long toes with long claws
for spikes

| 0 | 10 | 20 | 30 | 40 | 50 | 60 mph |

Throughout the age of dinosaurs there were species of ornithopods that were slender and ran solely on their hind legs. Is it possible to determine how fast these animals could run? Are there reliable clues?

There are three factors that must be considered. First, the length of the animal's legs — this can be measured using the bones found. Second, the body weight — this must be estimated. Third, the length of the animal's stride and its manner of walking — this information can be obtained by examining the body structure of the animal, and wherever possible, the fossilized footprints of its species. Present-day vertebrates that run at high speeds can be used as a comparison: race-horses and greyhounds, gazelles and cheetahs, hares and kangaroos, ostriches and roadrunners. The fastest ones are the cheetah and some species of gazelle, which can reach speeds of up to 60 miles per hour. What we see, is that medium-sized animals with a body weight around 110 pounds are the fastest runners. Both lighter and heavier animals are slower.

In the case of dinosaurs, these observations, together with data on leg lengths, tracks, and body weights, have enabled scientists to obtain the information summarized in the table shown above.

How fast could dinosaurs run?

COELOPHYSIS,

one of the first known dinosaurs of the Triassic period, must have been one of the fastest as well. It was very slim and lightly built, and weighed only about 66 pounds — despite being 9 feet long! Even some of the last dinosaurs — living at the end of the Cretaceous period, 150 million years after Coelophysis — were very slender, agile sprinters (see above).

Were dinosaurs warm-blooded?

COLD-BLOODED ANIMALS cannot maintain a set body temperature. Their body temperature depends on that of the environment. Lizards, for example, almost stop moving altogether in cold weather, which is why they look for a protective hiding-place in the fall. Only springtime temperatures draw them out again. In order to warm themselves up they lie in the sun. Only when they are warmed through and through are they agile and quick enough for a successful hunt.

WARM-BLOODED ANIMALS, however, can produce enough heat to maintain a steady body temperature. Except for the ones that hibernate, warm-blooded animals are active at all times of the year and are not dependent on seasonal temperatures or variations in the weather. Insulating feathers or hair protect them against excessive heat-loss.

Today's reptiles — snakes, lizards, crocodiles, and turtles — are multi-temperatured animals, often called simply cold-blooded. Their body temperature depends on that of the environment. Birds and mammals, on the other hand, can maintain a particular body temperature independent of the external temperature. Their bodies are able to create heat. This is why they are called warm-blooded animals.

Since dinosaurs are clearly reptiles, scientists used to think they were cold-blooded. Today, however, there are many signs that they had different kinds of warm-bloodedness. A predominantly warm and mild climate meant that the animals had a favorably high body temperature anyway. They could sun themselves if they needed more warmth. Some species had extended skin surface for this purpose: Spinosaurus and Ouranosaurus had "sails" on their backs and the stegosaurs had rows of large plates along their spines.

The huge bodies of the sauropods could not absorb enough heat in this way. In their case, however, muscle movements and the metabolic processes that occur in all living creatures generated enough inner warmth. Small bodies quickly lose this heat through the skin. In the large bodies of these giant dinosaurs, however, this loss was slowed by the long distance from the center of the animal to the skin, and by the relatively small surface area. As a result enough warmth collected so that the animals inevitably became warm-blooded.

Predatory dinosaurs developed a different kind of warm-bloodedness. The heat produced "incidentally" was supplemented by additionally warmth generated by their energy-rich, easily digested meat diet. As warm-blooded animals they were now ready at all times to chase prey or make a speedy escape.

The smaller species in particular must have lost a lot of heat through their skin. Therefore scientists assume that the smaller predatory dinosaurs had a layer of insulating feathers. There are even fossils to prove this in the case of Archaeopteryx, the ancestor of the birds.

The small predatory dinosaur Troodon may have had feathers.

What did dinosaur eggs look like?

The first remains of dinosaur eggs were found in the south of France in the 19th century. Since there were only fragments, it was impossible to be sure what species they belonged to or how big they had been. The first nest of complete eggs was discovered in the Gobi desert in 1923. They were from various species of dinosaur.

The site in southern France later turned out to be very productive. Researchers unearthed several hundred eggs that had been covered with sand and mud during a flood 70 million years ago. They distinguished ten different types of eggs. The largest eggs were roundish, up to 10 inches long, and held nearly a gallon of liquid. A dozen such eggs were found in a partially preserved nest about 3 feet wide and 28 inches deep. They were probably laid by the sauropod Hypselosaurus.

Did dinosaur parents care for their young?

The most spectacular finds of nests were made in Montana, in the years since 1978. A colony of more than ten duck-billed dinosaur nests was preserved there. Each nest was more than six feet wide and three feet deep. In one of them there were only crushed eggshells, but in another there were young animals between 20 and 80 inches long. At the time they hatched out of the eight-inch-long eggs they must have been about 12 to 14 inches long. Their size suggests that they must

Protoceratops eggs. They were found in the Gobi desert.

have stayed in the nest for quite a long time — which is how the shells got crushed — and were probably protected and fed by their mother. This species of duck-billed dinosaur was therefore called Maiasaura (= mother lizard). Considering that she weighed two tons it is unlikely that the mother actually incubated the eggs! The nests were made of plant material, and as it rotted it probably provided enough heat for incubation.

Nearby, gazelle dinosaurs had a nesting ground that seems to have been used for years. Up to 24 long eggs lay in the ten nests. Freshly hatched gazelle dinosaurs did not stay in the nest, however, but immediately left it and gathered in a nursery nearby.

Among the dinosaurs then, there were some whose young stayed in the nest and others whose young left the nest. The mother dinosaurs also looked after their young in different ways.

HOW LONG DID DINO-SAURS LIVE?

The simple method of determining the age of a living thing by counting the number of annual rings does not work for dinosaurs. These rings are caused by slowing of growth during cold seasons. Since the mild climate didn't change much during the year, dinosaurs were able to grow steadily. As a result neither the trees nor the teeth and

A herd of sauropods left their footprints here (Colorado, USA).

parallel to each other and only a few prints overlap. The different sizes of the footprint indicate that young animals also belonged to the herd and were herded along in the middle. A herd of duck-billed dinosaurs left footprints on a layer of rock in Canada. They were moving in a broad front across what was then soft ground. The young animals obviously trotted along behind as their tracks sometimes overlap those of the older animals. There are now many examples showing herbivores living in herds.

Some species of predatory dinosaurs also lived in packs. In one place scientists found 19 sets of tracks — from a species with a medium-sized stride — running side-by-side. This might mean that they also hunted in packs. In contrast, scientists have found only single tracks of large predatory dinosaurs such as Tyrannosaurus.

Did dinosaurs live in herds?

Discoveries of footprints and large collections of bones show that some dinosaur species lived in herds. An experienced tracker can glean a lot of information about the behavior of animals from their footprints.

On a layer of stone in Texas, 20 giant dinosaur tracks run

bones of dinosaurs developed distinct annual rings. Dinosaur lifespans are therefore a matter of guesswork.

Dinosaurs were capable of reproduction when they reached about two-thirds of their adult size. Growth then slowed down but it did not stop until death.

Duck-billed dinosaur mother with her young

The Other Saurians

The term "saurian" is sometimes

What is a saurian?

used ambiguously. Originally, it referred to all large reptiles and amphibians that lived in past ages and are now extinct. Nowadays, smaller species are also included in this family. Since the crocodiles, tuataras, and scaly lizards of the Mesozoic era are also described as saurians, one can include their surviving relatives too. In any case the term "saurian" means both "lizard" and "reptile." For example, a species might sometimes be called "armored lizard," and sometimes "armored saurian," and sometimes "armored reptile." The names all refer to the same species, however.

Anthracosaurians and armored amphibians are two saurians that we classify as amphibians today. It is very difficult to distinguish their skeletons from those of reptiles, however. One such species was Mastodonsaurus, for example, a giant 12-foot-long amphibian that lived like a crocodile in swamps and lakes.

THE THERIODONTS
(= "predator-toothed" reptiles) were mostly carnivores. Their shape and features became increasingly dog-like.

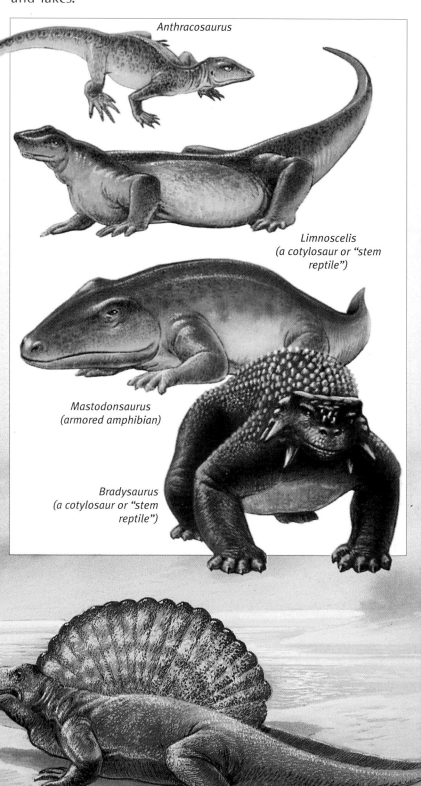

Anthracosaurus

*Limnoscelis
(a cotylosaur or "stem reptile")*

*Mastodonsaurus
(armored amphibian)*

*Bradysaurus
(a cotylosaur or "stem reptile")*

*Two pelycosaurs:
Dimetrodon (left) and
Edaphosaurus*

They probably developed the hair, lips, cheeks, mammary glands, and warm-bloodedness that later became typical of mammals.

Did other saurians exist before the dinosaurs?

The first reptiles, which developed during the Carboniferous period more than 300 million years ago, are called cotylosaurs or "stem reptiles." At first they were small, lizard-like predators. Over time they grew larger and relied more and more on vegetation as their source of food. The largest of these "stem" reptiles were about 9 feet long and slow-moving, with legs sprawling to the sides. They established themselves all across the earth, and are the ancestors of all reptiles.

The pelycosaurs, with their strong canine teeth and long tails, reached lengths of up to 9 feet. They evolved from the original reptiles as early as the Carboniferous period. Many of them had long bony quills extending from their backs and a "sail" of skin stretched between them.

The legs of a group called the therapsids — short-tailed mammal-like reptiles — gradually came to be situated below the body making walking easier, even for heavier animals. The heavy heads and fang-like canine teeth of the larger species of therapsids are reminiscent of the hippopotamus.

The theriodonts ("predator-toothed" reptiles) were mainly carnivores whose shape and features became increasingly dog-like. They probably developed features that later became typical of mammals.

Finally, there were the thecodonts ("socket-toothed" reptiles), the ancestors of the dinosaurs. The first thecodonts were similar to crocodiles and usually had an armor of bony plates beneath the skin. They developed an astonishing diversity. There were large-headed armored lizards, and long-snouted fish-catchers. There were tiny, 8-inch climbing lizards with parachute-like skin formations on their sides, and there were the slender, fast-running lizards that scientists think were the immediate ancestors of the dinosaurs.

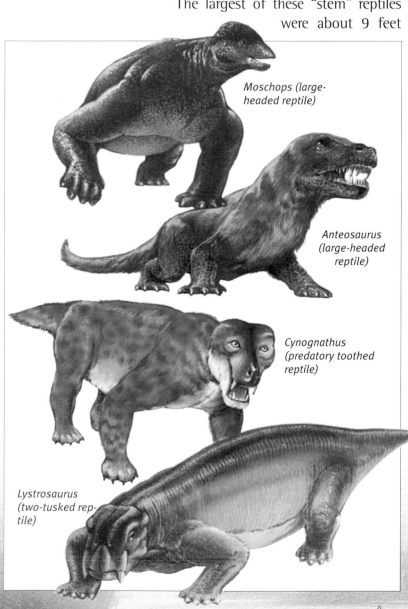

Moschops (large-headed reptile)

Anteosaurus (large-headed reptile)

Cynognathus (predatory toothed reptile)

Lystrosaurus (two-tusked reptile)

Two thecodonts: Desmatosuchus (left) and Longisquama

45

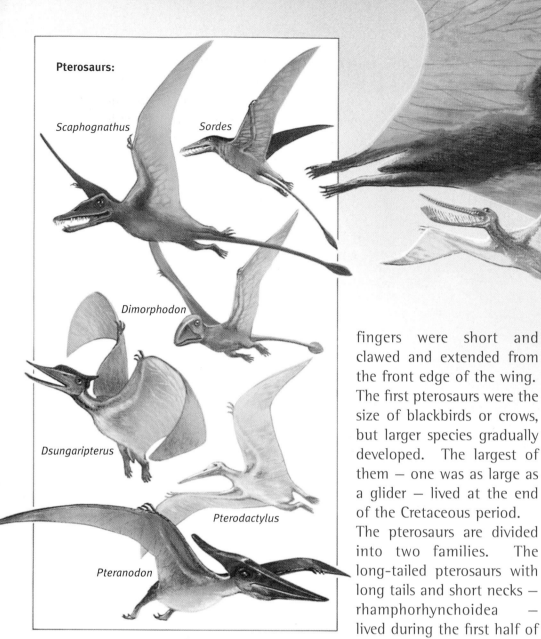

Pterosaurs:

Scaphognathus

Sordes

Dimorphodon

Dsungaripterus

Pterodactylus

Pteranodon

Quetzalcoatlus (top), the largest pterosaur, and the plankton-eating Pterodaustro.

The pterosaurs (= flying reptiles) lived at the same time as the dinosaurs. They both developed from the same ancestors, the thecodonts. What a difference there is, however, between the gigantic, elephant-footed dinosaurs and the delicate flying lizards! The pterosaurs' wing arms were their distinguishing trait. Thin leathery skin stretched from the side of the body to the tip of the hugely elongated fourth finger. The first three fingers were short and clawed and extended from the front edge of the wing. The first pterosaurs were the size of blackbirds or crows, but larger species gradually developed. The largest of them — one was as large as a glider — lived at the end of the Cretaceous period.

Which saurians could fly?

The pterosaurs are divided into two families. The long-tailed pterosaurs with long tails and short necks — rhamphorhynchoidea — lived during the first half of the age of dinosaurs, until the end of the Jurassic period. The short-tailed pterosaurs with longer necks and thinner, longer wings — pterodactyloidea — first appeared as the long-tailed pterosaurs were dying out. They survived until the end of the Cretaceous period.

Most pterosaurs ate fish. Scientists learned this by examining food remains they found in the stomach or throat areas in fossil specimens. Flying low over the water they would use their snouts, and the sharp teeth inside them, to snatch up fish to feed on.

THE LARGEST pterosaurs had no teeth but only a horny beak. Pteranodon (= toothless flier) may have plowed through the water with the bottom part of its beak and then snapped it shut when it snared a fish. Smaller species presumably ate insects, and the largest ptero-saur of all — Quetzalcoatlus — probably lived on carrion like present-day vultures.

ICHTHYOSAURUS

(= "fish saurian" or "fish reptile") probably gave birth to live young. Scientists confirmed this theory when they discovered well-preserved skeletons of pregnant females with fully developed young animals in their bellies.

What did the sea saurians look like?

Most saurians lived on land, but several families made the sea their permanent home and effectively adapted their bodies to this environment:

1. Placodus (or plaster-toothed reptile) and Nothosaurus were lizard-shaped and had oar-like feet and a laterally flattened, oar-like tail.

2. Sea crocodiles and mosasaurs developed an elongated shape that was propelled forward solely by the waving, serpentine motion of their oar-shaped tails.

3. Plesiosaurs, pliosaurs, and sea turtles were shaped like paddling lizards and used only their fin-like legs to propel themselves.

4. The dolphin-like ichthyosaurs had the shape of fish and were propelled forwards by short movements of the tall tail fin.

All the major species crossbred, which resulted in a huge variety of sea reptiles. The ichthyosaurs (= fish reptiles) show the most divergence from the four-legged, land-based lizard shape of the first reptiles. The original five-toed feet became flat, lateral fins. Because of their fish-like shape, these reptiles could no longer lay their eggs on land, as was typical of the other sea reptiles and present-day turtles. So ichthyosaurs must have given birth to live animals!

Ichthyosaurus, an ichthyosaur or "fish" reptile.

Geosaurus, a sea crocodile.

Sea reptiles:

Sea turtle

Placodus (plaster-toothed reptile)

Nothosaurus

Kronosaurus (a Pliosaur)

Plesiosaurus

Mosasaurus

Adriosaurus, a mosasaur.

The End of the Dinosaurs

When did the dinosaurs die out?

This question is often answered quickly and simply: about 65 million years ago at the end of the Cretaceous period and thus at the end of the Mesozoic Era. New species of dinosaurs had dominated life on land for over 150 million years and then within a short time disappeared completely from the surface of the Earth. Not a single dinosaur has been found in the fossils of the Tertiary period.

Not all dinosaur species or families survived even this long. The forerunners of the giant sauropods had already died out 120 million years before, in the middle of the age of dinosaurs. The stegosaurs became extinct 60 million years before the other types of dinosaurs. On the other hand, the pachycephalosaurs and ceratopsians first made their appearance at this time.

New species were constantly developing, but at the same time many also disappeared totally. Most dinosaur species existed for "only" two million years though some survived for as long as ten million years!

Why did the dinosaurs die out?

Ever since dinosaurs were discovered, over 150 years ago, scientists have been trying to find out what caused the total extinction of the dinosaurs at the end of the Cretaceous period.

Skeleton of a Brachiosaurus at the Natural History Museum in Berlin, Germany. They were already extinct 140 million years ago.

Triceratops died out 65 million years ago.

YET WE DO NOT KNOW EXACTLY why the dinosaurs disappeared. Most theories have overlooked the fact that many types of animals survived whatever it was that drove the dinosaurs to extinction. When the dinosaurs disappeared, so did the sea saurians, ammonites, and other small sea creatures — as well as many land plants. Crocodiles, lizards, snakes, turtles, birds, and mammals, on the other hand, survived.

THEORIES ABOUT a legendary flood are nonsense — whatever happened, many sea creatures also died out while many land animals were not harmed. Theories suggesting that primitive man exterminated them are likewise nonsense — since man did not appear until 60 million years after the last dinosaurs!

OTHER REASONS having to do with the dinosaurs themselves cannot be the only cause either. The enormous size and the clumsiness of some dinosaurs does not explain their extinction, since the smallest and the fastest of dinosaurs also died out.

More than a hundred theories about the causes of their disappearance have been proposed, though most have been shown to be invalid.

One of the most recent theories claims there was a sudden catastrophe caused by the impact of a huge meteorite. According to this theory, a meteorite with a diameter of about six miles collided with the Earth. The impact blew so much dust into the air that the sky was darkened over the whole planet for several months. The plants that depended on light died and the plant-eaters with them, and finally the meat-eaters. First it became very cold, since sunlight could no longer reach the surface of the Earth. Later it became very hot, since the higher layers of air — above the dust clouds — would have heated up enormously in the meantime. If any species of dinosaur survived this, they died later from after-effects that lasted for years and even centuries.

If this catastrophe really occurred — and there is a lot of evidence that it did — the sudden extinction of all dinosaurs would be quite understandable. On the other hand, it would be hard to explain why other sensitive animals, such as birds, survived!

More convincing research indicates that the extinction of the dinosaurs was not sudden but took place over a longer-lasting period of crisis. Living conditions gradually deteriorated for those animals that had adapted to a climate that had been uniformly humid and warm until this point. They had also grown accustomed to a luxuriant plant and animal life. Constant shifts of the continents and seas brought about noticeable climatic changes. The movement of the earth's crust and the expansion of the deeper parts of the oceans caused more and more shallow marine regions to become dry land with less luxuriant plant growth. Furthermore, cooler nights and colder winters interrupted the usual warm temperatures.

Many dinosaurs were no longer able to find ample food whenever and wherever they needed it. The cool nights and winters worsened incubation conditions for eggs. Young animals grew more slowly. Individual species of dinosaur gradually became rarer and slowly died out, faster in one area, slower in another. This time of crisis lasted at least 5 million years on land, where not only dinosaurs and pterosaurs but also certain species of plants and mammals were becoming rarer and rarer. At the same time, however, other plant and mammal species came into being and spread.

A collision with a meteorite or some other sudden catastrophe could have aggravated unfavorable conditions for the plant and animal kingdoms, but it could not have been the main reason for their decline.

Index